I Miss You, Stinky Face

Written by:
Lisa McCourt

Illustrated by:
Cyd Moore

Cartwheel
·B·O·O·K·S·®

SCHOLASTIC INC.

New York   Toronto   London   Auckland   Sydney
Mexico City   New Delhi   Hong Kong   Buenos Aires

For Tucker...LM. For Ran and Jay...CM.

ISBN 0-439-63470-9

Text copyright © 1999 by Lisa McCourt.
Illustrations copyright © 1999 by Cyd Moore.
All rights reserved. Published by Scholastic Inc.
SCHOLASTIC, CARTWHEEL BOOKS, and associated logos
are trademarks and/or registered trademarks of Scholastic Inc.

First published in hardcover by BridgeWater Books.
Produced by Boingo Books, Inc.

10 9 8 7 6 5 4 3 2 1   04 05 06 07 08

Printed in the U.S.A.   08

First Scholastic printing, October 2003

"I miss you, my little Stinky Face," said Mama on the phone.
But I had a question.

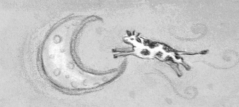

Mama, do you miss me so much that you're coming right home to me, no matter what?

"I'm coming today," said Mama, "on a big silver airplane."

But, Mama, but, Mama, what if the airplane forgets how to fly?

"If that airplane forgets how to fly, I'll hop in the basket of a hot-air balloon. I'll soar past clouds and stars until I see your window, then I'll float right into your room."

But, Mama, what if the balloon runs out of hot air and you have to land in the middle of the desert?

"If I have to land in the middle of the desert, I'll climb up on a camel and ride him like a racehorse all the way home."

But, Mama, but, Mama, what if the camel gets so tired that he just won't take another step and he leaves you stranded in the jungle?

"Then I'll search that jungle for a cheetah, the fastest animal there is. I'll jump on her back, and she'll race me straight home to you."

"But, Mama, what if the cheetah doesn't want to leave the jungle?"

"If the cheetah doesn't want to leave the jungle, I'll hunt down some pirates digging for buried treasure and ask them to sail me home to you on their big scary ship."

But, Mama, what if the terrible pirates make you walk the gangplank?

"Then I'll find the speediest shark in the ocean. I'll grab on to his fin and use it to steer, and we'll skim through the high seas all the way home to you."

"If the shark tries that, I'll leap from his greedy jaws and body surf to shore. I'll call the bravest astronauts and hitch a ride on their supersonic spaceship, and we'll all be home to you faster than the speed of light."

"If the spaceship lands that far back in time, I'll look around for a magic dragon.

"I'll climb way up on her back
and whisper in her ear just
how much I miss you.
The magic dragon will fly me
through time right back to you."

But, Mama, where would such a big magic dragon land?

"I think there's enough room on the driveway if you make
sure your bike's put away."

I'll put it away.... But, Mama, the airplane is
how you'll probably come home, right?

"Probably."

I miss you, Mama.

"And I miss you, my little Stinky Face."